This book is dedicated to all of you who have been waiting patiently for this collection of recipes as well as Harry, Luckythedog, Daizy, The Cheese, Foxx and Alice. They have been the best clean up crew in recorded history.

I have always thought that food is something to celebrate. The idea of it has been lost to many people over the years. With our busy schedules and longer work days, eating out or grabbing something quick became the norm as opposed to a special occasion.

For me, going out to enjoy a meal has always been a celebration and I've taken that passion and put it into preparing something wonderful in my own kitchen. I prefer the latter of course, simply because I can control the consistency of each dish thats served as well as the company you keep. Luckily, I'm not alone in my adoration of an exceptional meal and the interest in cooking at home is back on the rise.

Heck, as the world becomes a much smaller planet, you can have the vanilla beans you ordered from Madagascar, at your doorstep the very next day!

Aside from sustaining life, food has sealed the deal on a number of proposals, business endeavors and just plain old bringing people together. Autumn, 2011 marked the first in a series of on going classes offered in my quaint little kitchen in Shadow Hills, California. The curriculum was simple, whatever you like to dine out, I'll show you how to dine in.

The group consisted of old and new friends and every week the excitement built. Some didn't even know how to chop an onion when we started, but by the end there were only the important questions left...Is it good? What wine goes with it? Do you want ice cream with dessert?

The Sunflower is a cottage industry boutique bakery offering an online bake shop, catering, personal chef service and cooking classes in and around the greater Los Angeles County area. Looking forward, we will soon establish a brick and mortar location which would include a small cafe area and a more functional space to meet the increased demand from our customers which includes cooking classes, personal chef service and special events promoting local Artisan Products. We plan to showcase local brew-masters and wine makers as well as using all local, seasonal ingredients when available. Whatever it is, I strive to be consistent by making sure everyone enjoys their experience. Whether they are just picking up a torte or they are on a first date, if it's food by "The Sunflower, it's definitely something to celebrate. I hope you enjoy this first collection of recipes from that special cooking class. Maybe well see you at the shop one day soon!

Chapter One

COMFORT FOOD

In its purest definition, comfort food is food prepared in a traditional style having a nostalgic or sentimental appeal.

This chapter will explore just that; our go-to dishes that evoke comfort, warmth and home well, my home; a really delicious place to be.

Croque Monsieur

A Parisian favorite. Mine too!

Whatcha Need:

2 tbsps unsalted butter
3 tbsps all-purpose flour
2 cups hot milk
1 tsp kosher salt
1/2 tsp freshly ground black pepper
Pinch nutmeg
12 ounces Gruyere, grated (5 cups)
1/2 cup freshly grated Parmesan
16 slices white sandwich bread, crusts removed
Dijon mustard
8 ounces baked Virginia ham, sliced but not paper thin

How To Do It:

Preheat the oven to 400 degrees F. Melt the butter over low heat in a small saucepan and add the flour all at once, stirring with a wooden spoon for 2 minutes. Slowly pour the hot milk into the butter flour mixture and cook, whisking constantly, until the sauce is thickened. Off the heat add the salt, pepper, nutmeg, 1/2 cup grated Gruyere, and the Parmesan and set aside.

To toast the bread, place the slices on 2 baking sheets and bake for 5 minutes. Turn each slice and bake for another 2 minutes, until toasted. Lightly brush half the toasted breads with mustard, add a slice of ham to each, and sprinkle with half the remaining Gruyere. Top with another piece of toasted bread. Slather the tops with the cheese sauce, sprinkle with the remaining Gruyere, and bake the sandwiches for 5 minutes.

Turn on the broiler and broil for 3 to 5 minutes, or until the topping is bubbly and lightly browned. Serve hot.

Chicken Pot Pie

Yum.

How To Do It:

To make the sauce and vegetables, in a large frying pan, melt 1 Tbs. of the butter over medium heat. Add the mushrooms and cook, stirring occasionally, until they begin to brown, about 6 minutes. Stir in the leeks and carrots, cover and cook, stirring occasionally, until the leeks are tender, about 5 minutes. Remove from the heat and stir in the peas.

In a large saucepan, melt the remaining 5 Tbs. butter over medium-low heat. Whisk in the flour and let bubble gently for 1 minute. Gradually whisk in the stock and brandy and then the tarragon. Bring to a boil, whisking frequently. Stir in the shredded chicken and the mushroom-leek mixture and season with salt and pepper. Let cool until lukewarm, about 1/2 hour.

Preheat an oven to 400°F. Spoon the chicken mixture into six 1 1/2-cup ovenproof soup crocks, ramekins a 9" pie plate. Place the unwrapped dough on a lightly floured work surface and dust the top with flour. (If the dough is chilled hard, let it stand at room temperature for a few minutes until it begins to soften before rolling it out.)

For the soup crocks or ramekins, roll it out into a rectangle about 20 by 13 inches and 1/8 inch thick. Using a 6-inch saucer as a template, use a knife to cut out 6 rounds. For 9" pie plate, roll dough in a 10 – 12" circle. Beat the egg with a pinch of salt. Lightly brush each round with the egg .. doing the same if making a 9" pie.

Place dough egg side down, keeping the pastry taut and pressing it around the edges to adhere. Lightly brush the tops with the egg. Bake until the pastry is puffed and golden brown, about 25 minutes. Transfer each ramekin to a dinner plate and serve. Serves 6.

You can also use biscuit dough in place of the pastry dough. Roll out the dough 1/2 inch thick, then cut out rounds to fit just inside the rim of each ramekin. Bake at 400°F until the biscuit topping is golden brown, about 20 minutes.

Whatcha Need:

6 tablespoons unsalted butter
1/2 lb. button mushrooms, quartered
1 cup chopped leeks, white and pale green parts
1/2 cup finely diced carrots
1/3 cup fresh or thawed frozen peas
1/3 cup plus 1 Tbs. all-purpose flour
4 1/2 cups chicken stock
1/3 cup dry sherry/ brandy
2 tsp. minced fresh tarragon
4 cups shredded cooked chicken
Kosher salt and freshly ground pepper
Old Faithful pie crust for a double-crust pie (see Desserts, Chapter 4)
1 large egg

Chicken n' Dumplings

Chicken and dumplings, like most southern food, evolved out of necessity and practicality. Back in the day, chicken was a treat and not something offered or even available on a regular basis.

Whatcha Need:

8 boneless, skinless chicken breasts
salt and pepper to taste
Box of Bisquick (yep, thats right)
1/2 cup Milk
2 or 3 tsp. butter

How To Do It:
Place chicken breasts in a large soup pot and cover with water (fill the pot about half full). Add salt and pepper to taste. Cook over medium-high heat until chicken is done. Remove chicken and cut into bite sized pieces. Place chicken pieces back in broth. Simmer chicken and broth on low while making dumplings.

Using the Bisquick and milk, prepare as much dumpling mix as you want (as many as your pot will hold) according to package instructions. Coat your hands with flour, sprinkle a little flour on top of the dumpling mix, and roll dumplings into 1 inch balls. Add a little more flour when dumpling mix begins to get too sticky to roll. When you're almost finished rolling the dumplings, turn up the heat under the chicken and broth and bring to a slow boil. Drop dumplings into boiling broth.

Make sure they submerge. They'll pop back up, but you need to make sure they get totally wet. Once all dumplings are in the broth, add 1/2 cup milk and 2 or 3 tsps butter and poke all the dumplings down again. Do not stir before the dumplings are cooked, because it will tear them up.

Simmer for about 10-15 minutes, stirring occasionally but gently (if all dumplings appear to be cooked) to make sure chicken doesn't stick to bottom of pot.

Sweet Potato Fries

Maybe a new Thanksgiving favorite!

Whatcha Need:

6 sweet medium size potatoes, cut into
French fries strips
2 tbsps canola oil
3 tbsps taco seasoning mix
1/4 tsp cayenne pepper

How To Do It:

Preheat the oven to 425 degrees F (220 degrees C). In a zip-lock plastic bag combine the sweet potatoes, canola oil, taco seasoning, and cayenne pepper. Close and shake the bag until the fries are evenly coated. Spread the fries out in a single layer on two large baking sheets. Bake for 30 minutes, or until crispy and brown on one side. Turn the fries over using a spatula, and cook for another 30 minutes, or until they are all crispy on the outside and tender inside. Thinner fries may not take as long.

Turkey Chili

More flavor, less fat!

Whatcha Need:
1/4 cup olive oil, divided
3 cups chopped yellow onions
3/4 cup diced red bell pepper
3/4 cup diced green bell pepper
2 jalapeno peppers, seeded and minced
1 1/2 tbsps minced garlic
3 pounds ground turkey
1/4 cup finely chopped cilantro stems
2 1/2 tbsps chili powder
2 tsps unsweetened cocoa powder
2 tsps ground cumin
1 1/2 tsps salt, or to taste
3/4 tsp crumbled Mexican oregano
1/2 tsp sugar
1/4 tsp crushed red pepper
1 (28-ounce) can diced tomatoes with their juices
1 (8-ounce) can tomato sauce
6 cups chicken broth
1 1/2 cups cooked and drained kidney beans
1 1/2 cups cooked and drained black beans
1/4 cup finely chopped cilantro leaves

How To Do It:

Heat 2 tbsp of the oil in a 4 quart large, heavy saucepan and, when hot, add the onions and both the red and green bell peppers and cook until vegetables are soft and lightly caramelized, about 6 minutes. Add the jalapeños and garlic and cook until fragrant, 1 to 2 minutes. Add the remaining 2 tbsps of oil and the turkey, cilantro stems, chili powder, cocoa powder, cumin, salt, oregano, sugar, and crushed red pepper and cook, stirring to break up any lumps, until the turkey is cooked through and the spices are very fragrant, about 6 minutes. Add the tomatoes, tomato sauce, and chicken broth and bring to a boil. Reduce heat to a simmer and cook for 20 minutes. Add the kidney beans and black beans and cook until the flavors come together and the chili has thickened, about 30 minutes longer. Add the cilantro, remove from the heat and let sit for 10 minutes before serving. Server in bowls with some shredded cheddar cheese and sour cream (if you like it!).

Grown Up Mac n' Cheese

Whatcha Need:

2 tbsps olive oil
1/3 cup diced pancetta
1/2 cup small-diced onion
1 tsp minced garlic
2 tbsps butter
5 tbsps all-purpose flour
3 cups half-and-half or milk
3/4 tsp salt
1/2 tsp white pepper
1/2 tsp fresh ground nutmeg
1 pound small shell pasta, cooked al dente
4 ounces grated Parmigiano-Reggiano
4 ounces grated white Cheddar 4 ounces grated Gruyere
4 ounces grated Fontina
1/4 cup bread crumbs

How To Do It:

Preheat the oven to 350 degrees F. Set a large, wide-mouthed 6-quart pot over medium heat. Add the olive oil and pancetta to the pot and cook the pancetta until lightly browned, 3 to 4 minutes. Add the onions and garlic to the pan and cook until translucent, 3 to 4 minutes. Add the butter and flour to the pot and cook, stirring, for 3 minutes. Add the half-and-half to the pot and whisk until smooth.

Bring to a boil then reduce the heat to a simmer. Season with the salt, white pepper and nutmeg and cook for 3 minutes. Add the pasta to the pot and remove from the heat. Add the grated cheeses to the pot and stir to combine well. Transfer the contents of the pot to a 3-quart baking dish.

In a small bowl, combine the bread crumbs with the Essence and sprinkle over the top of the macaroni. Bake uncovered until golden brown and bubbling, 40 to 45 minutes.

Stuffed Pork Rolls with Prosciutto

Whatcha Need:

2 tbsps olive oil
1/3 cup diced pancetta
1/2 cup small-diced onion
1 tsp minced garlic
2 tbsps butter
5 tbsps all-purpose flour
3 cups half-and-half or milk
3/4 tsp salt
1/2 tsp white pepper
1/2 tsp fresh ground nutmeg
1 pound small shell pasta, cooked al dente
4 ounces grated Parmigiano-Reggiano
4 ounces grated white Cheddar 4 ounces grated Gruyere
4 ounces grated Fontina
1/4 cup bread crumbs

How To Do It:

Preheat the oven to 350 degrees F. Set a large, wide-mouthed 6-quart pot over medium heat. Add the olive oil and pancetta to the pot and cook the pancetta until lightly browned, 3 to 4 minutes. Add the onions and garlic to the pan and cook until translucent, 3 to 4 minutes. Add the butter and flour to the pot and cook, stirring, for 3 minutes. Add the half-and-half to the pot and whisk until smooth. Bring to a boil then reduce the heat to a simmer. Season with the salt, white pepper and nutmeg and cook for 3 minutes. Add the pasta to the pot and remove from the heat. Add the grated cheeses to the pot and stir to combine well. Transfer the contents of the pot to a 3-quart baking dish. In a small bowl, combine the bread crumbs with the Essence and sprinkle over the top of the macaroni. Bake uncovered until golden brown and bubbling, 40 to 45 minutes.

Bacon Cheddar Biscuits

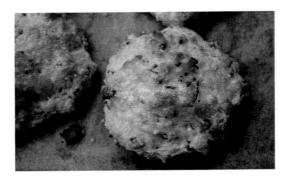

Yes, that's correct... Bacon, cheddar and biscuits!

Whatcha Need:

6 oz. bacon, diced
2 cups unbleached flour
1 Tbs. baking powder
1 tsp. kosher salt
2 tsp. sugar
3/4 tsp. freshly ground pepper
8 Tbs. (1 stick) cold unsalted butter, cut into 8 pieces, plus 2 Tbs. melted butter
3/4 cup shredded extra-sharp cheddar cheese
1/4 cup grated Parmigiano- Reggiano cheese
3/4 cup plus 2 tbs. buttermilk

How To Do It:

Preheat an oven to 425F. In an 11-inch fry pan over medium-high heat, cook the bacon, stirring occasionally, until crisp, about 10 minutes. Using a slotted spoon, transfer the bacon to a paper towel-lined plate. Discard all but 1 Tbs. of the fat in the pan. Using a pastry brush, spread the fat evenly over the pan bottom. Finely chop the bacon. Set aside. In a large bowl, whisk together the flour, baking powder, salt, sugar and pepper. Using a pastry blender or 2 knives, cut in the cold butter until pea-size crumbs form, then use your fingers to pinch the crumbs into flat disks. Stir in the cheddar and Parmigiano-Reggiano cheeses and the bacon. Stir in the buttermilk until the dough just comes together. Transfer the dough to a floured work surface and roll out into a 9 1/2-by-11-inch rectangle. Fold the dough into thirds, rotate 90 degrees and roll out into the same-size rectangle. Fold into thirds again, rotate 90 degrees and roll out into a 7-by-9 1/2-inch rectangle about 12 inch (12mm) thick.

Using a floured 2 1/2-inch biscuit cutter, cut out biscuits and place in the fry pan. Gather up the scraps, re-roll the dough and cut out more biscuits. You should have 9 biscuits around the circumference of the pan and 3 in the center. Brush the tops of the biscuits with the melted butter. Bake the biscuits until golden brown and a toothpick inserted into the center comes out clean, 20 to 25 minutes. Let cool for 10 minutes before serving. Makes 12 biscuits.

Panini

You can make all kinds of different Panini combinations... This is the roast turkey and Swiss.

Whatcha Need:

2 tbsps fat-free mayonnaise
4 tsps basil pesto
8 (1-ounce) thin slices sourdough bread
8 ounces sliced roast turkey breast
2 ounces thinly sliced Swiss cheese
8 (1/8-inch-thick) slices tomato
1 bunch fresh basil (makes enough for 4 Panini)

How To Do It:

Combine mayonnaise and pesto, stirring well. Spread 1 tbsp mayonnaise mixture on each of 4 bread slices; top each slice with 2 ounces turkey, 1/2 ounce cheese, and 2 tomato slices. Top with remaining bread slices. Preheat grill pan, large nonstick skillet coated with cooking spray over medium heat.

Add sandwiches to pan; top with another heavy skillet. Cook 3 minutes on each side or until golden brown. (If you have a Panini press then heck! All the better!)

Repeat process for the number of Panini you need. Garnish with a basil leaf.

Chicken Marsala

Whatcha need:

1 3/4 cups reduced-sodium chicken broth (14 fl oz)
2 tbsp finely chopped shallot
5 tbsp unsalted butter
10 oz mushrooms, trimmed and thinly sliced
1/2 cup black olives, pitted (yes, I put olives in this one)
1 1/2 tsps finely chopped fresh sage
1/4 tsp salt
1/8 tsp black pepper
1 cup all-purpose flour
4 skinless boneless chicken breast halves (2 lb total)
2 tbsps extra-virgin olive oil
1/2 cup plus 2 tbs dry Marsala wine
2/3 cup heavy cream
1 tsp fresh lemon juice

How to do it:

Put oven rack in middle position and preheat oven to 200F.
Bring broth to a boil in a 2-quart saucepan over high heat, then boil, uncovered, until reduced to about 3/4 cup, about 20 minutes. Cook shallot in 3 tbsps butter in an 8- to 10-inch heavy skillet over moderate heat, stirring, until shallot begins to turn golden, about 1 minute. Add mushrooms, 1 tsp sage, salt, and pepper and cook, stirring occasionally, until liquid mushrooms give off is evaporated and mushrooms begin to brown, 6 to 8 minutes. Remove from heat. Put flour in a wide shallow bowl. Gently pound chicken to 1/4 inch thick between 2 sheets of plastic wrap using the flat side of a meat pounder or a rolling pin.

Pat chicken dry and season with salt and pepper, then dredge in flour, 1 piece at a time, shaking off excess. Transfer to sheets of wax paper, arranging chicken in 1 layer.

Heat 1 tbsp each of oil and butter in a 10-inch heavy skillet over moderately high heat until foam
subsides, then sauté half of chicken, turning over once, until golden and just cooked through, about 4 minutes total. Transfer cooked chicken to a large heatproof platter, arranging in 1 layer, then put platter in oven to keep warm. Add 1/2 cup wine to skillet and boil over high heat, stirring and scraping up brown bits, about 30 seconds.

Add reduced broth, cream, and mushrooms, then simmer, stirring occasionally, until sauce is slightly thickened, 6 to 8 minutes. Add lemon juice and remaining 2 tbs wine and 1/2 tsp sage. Serve chicken with sauce.

Double Stuffed Baked Potato

Whatcha Need:

4 Medium size Russet potatoes
2 tbsp extra virgin olive oil
3 tbsp unsalted butter, melted (make sure its unsalted butter trust me, there IS a difference!)
1/2 cup sour cream
2 cups grated, sharp cheddar cheese, divided
2 cups steamed broccoli, roughly chopped
1/2 tsp onion powder
1/4 cup warmed milk (and by warmed I mean you can put your finger in it without getting a second degree burn)
Salt and ground black pepper to taste (I like lots of pepper and sometimes even divide the pepper up as half black pepper and half red pepper flakes its how I roll).

How To Do It:

Preheat the oven to 425F. With a fork, poke some holes all over the potatoes and give them a nice olive oil massage. Bake on a foil or sil-mat covered cookie sheet for about an hour then let them cool down for 15 minutes (if youre in a hurry you can always run the cooked potatoes under cold water until cool enough to handle).
Slice the potatoes in half and scoop out the potato-ie goodness into a large bowl, taking care not too puncture the potato skin.

Mash together with butter, sour cream, cooked broccoli and 1 cups of cheddar. Mix in the onion powder then season with salt and pepper. Mix the milk in and boom. Ready to stuff those skins!

There should be enough filling for all 8 of the potato halves sprinkle remaining cheddar on top of each potato half and bake for 20 minutes more. Nom, nom, nom.

Chapter Two

PARTY APPETIZERS

It doesn't have to take weeks to plan a party. What it does take is having a few crowd pleasing go-tos in the appetizer department. I've pulled together the successful ones from our Thursday night cooking classes we spent 7 classes on party food.

We are ready for anything!

Cilantro & Lime Skewers

Works with pork loin, shrimp and veggies too!

Whatcha Need:

1 package of boneless, skinless chicken breasts (about 2 lbs)
1 bunch of cilantro
1 cup of lime juice
1/4 cup of extra virgin olive oil
A good shake of red pepper flakes
salt and pepper to taste

How To Do It:

Soak a package of bamboo skewers in warm water for about a half hour. Remember to pre-heat the grill to medium/high. Cut chicken into 1 & inch strips and thread onto each skewer and cook on the grill until they are cooked through, about 4 minutes each side.

Meanwhile, combine all the rest of the ingredients in a food processor or, if you have one, an emulsifier cup and process until the cilantro is thoroughly mixed into the liquid. Pour over plated skewers and serve. (keep some of the liquid in reserve for dipping! Yum!)

7 Layer Dip

This is also known as "the dip". It's a huge crowd pleaser and has a permanent spot at all my gatherings.

Whatcha Need:

2 pkg's Taco Seasoning
2 16 oz cans refried black beans
2 8 oz cans (yep, cans...) sliced black olives
2 8 oz cans diced green chili peppers
1 bag shredded cheddar cheese
2 bunches green onions (aka scallions, chopped on the diagonal)
1 X 24oz container sour cream

How To Do It:

In a lasagna sized pan start with the beans on the bottom and layer as follows: Beans Taco seasoning Green chilis' (make sure they are drained really well) Olives (drained) Green onions Sour cream Cheddar cheese Put in 350F oven (uncovered) for 45 minutes or until it starts to bubble underneath the cheese layer. Serve with crusty bread or tortilla chips!

Grilled Bacon Jalapeno Wraps

Bacon, cheese and the spicy zing of a jalapeño pepper. This is the perfect finger food.

Whatcha Need:

6 fresh jalapeño peppers, halved lengthwise and seeded
1 (8 ounce) package cream cheese
(*note: you can use low moisture mozzarella as well)
12 slices bacon

How To Do It:

Preheat an outdoor grill for high heat. Spread cream cheese to fill jalapeno halves. Wrap with bacon. Secure with a toothpick. Place on the grill, and cook until bacon is crispy.

Gorgonzola Profiteroles

Whatcha Need:

1/2 cup hazelnuts
1 cup milk
1 stick plus 1 tbsp unsalted butter
2 tbsps Frangelico or other nut flavored liqueur
2 tsps sugar
3/4 tsp salt
1 cup all-purpose flour
4 large eggs
1 large egg yolk mixed with 2 tbsp of water
1/4 pound blue cheese, such as Maytag, at room temperature
1/2 cup mascarpone
1/2 cup heavy cream
Seedless red grapes, for serving

How To Do It:

Preheat the oven to 375 and position racks in the upper and middle thirds. Line 2 large baking sheets with parchment paper. Spread the hazelnuts in a pie plate and toast for about 12 minutes, until the nuts are fragrant and the skins are blistered. Transfer the nuts to a clean kitchen towel and rub vigorously to remove the skins. Let the hazelnuts cool completely.

Transfer the hazelnuts to a food processor and finely grind them. In a large saucepan, combine the milk with the butter, Frangelico, sugar and salt and bring to a simmer over moderate heat. Remove from the heat. Add the flour and 1/4 cup plus 2 tbsps of the ground hazelnuts and stir with a wooden spoon until a mass forms. Return the saucepan to moderate heat and cook the dough, stirring, for 1 minute. Transfer the dough to a medium bowl and let it cool for 2 minutes.

Using an electric mixer, beat in the eggs one at a time, beating well between additions. Transfer the dough to a pastry bag fitted with a 1/2-inch plain tip. Pipe 1 inch mounds of the dough onto the prepared baking sheets, about 1 inch apart. Brush the tops with the egg wash and sprinkle with the remaining ground hazelnuts. Bake for about 25 minutes, until the profiteroles are puffed and golden; shift the pans from top to bottom and front to back halfway through baking.

Poke a hole in the side of each puff to release the steam. Let the puffs cool completely. In a medium bowl, using an electric mixer, beat the blue cheese with the mascarpone and heavy cream at medium speed until firm and fluffy.

Using a serrated knife, split each puff horizontally and remove any doughy centers with a spoon Fill each puff with 1/2 tbsp of the blue cheese cream and replace the tops. Transfer to a platter and serve with the grapes. MAKE AHEAD The filling can be refrigerated for up to 4 hours. The baked puffs can be covered and stored at room temperature for up to 2 days. Re-crisp in the oven before splitting, filling and serving.

Egg Plant Tapenade

A spin on the old stand by, olive tapenade. The eggplant adds a surprising depth to this one!

Whatcha Need:

1 baguette
4 tbsps extra-virgin olive oil
1 1/2 garlic cloves, whole clove left unpeeled
1 small eggplant (1/2 lb)
1/2 tsp finely chopped fresh thyme
1/4 tsp finely chopped fresh rosemary
1/4 tsp finely chopped fresh oregano
/4 tsp coarse gray sea salt
1/8 tsp coarsely ground black pepper
1 tbsp chopped fresh flat-leaf parsley
2 tbsps finely grated Parmigiano-Reggiano

How To Do It:

Put oven rack in middle position and preheat oven to 375F. Cut off and discard 1 end of baguette, then cut 12 (1/4-inch-thick) crosswise slices from baguette (reserve remainder for another use).
Lightly brush 1 side of each slice with some oil (about 1 tbsp total) and arrange, oiled sides up, on a baking sheet. Toast until golden, 8 to 10 minutes. While toasts are still warm, rub oiled sides with cut side of garlic clove half, then transfer to a rack to cool. Reduce oven temperature to 350F. Halve eggplant lengthwise and make shallow 1/2-inch-long incisions all over cut sides with tip of a paring knife. Arrange eggplant, cut sides up (without crowding), in a shallow baking dish and add unpeeled garlic clove.

Sprinkle thyme, rosemary, oregano, sea salt, and pepper over eggplant, then drizzle eggplant and garlic with 2 tbsps oil. Bake until garlic is very tender, 30 to 35 minutes, then transfer garlic to a cutting board and continue to bake eggplant until very tender, 20 to 25 minutes more. When garlic is cool enough to handle, squeeze flesh from peel onto cutting board.
Transfer eggplant to cutting board and let stand until cool enough to handle, about 15 minutes. Scrape out flesh with a spoon onto cutting board, discarding peel.

Finely chop eggplant and garlic together and transfer to a bowl. Add parsley and remaining tbsp oil, then stir until combined well. Season with sea salt and pepper to taste. Top toasts with eggplant mixture and more cheese!

Guacamole

Everyone needs to have a solid guac recipe in their arsenal. Here's mine.

Whatcha Need:

4 ripe, fresh California avocados, peeled and seeded
1/2 tsp ground cumin
1 ripe, medium Roma tomato, seeded, diced
1/2 cup minced sweet white onion
2 serrano chilies, seeded and minced
1/2 cup cilantro leaves, chopped
4 Tbsp. fresh lime juice
Hot pepper sauce
Sea salt, to taste
White pepper, to taste

How To Do It:

Cut avocado in large chunks and mash coarsely in large bowl with a fork.
Add remaining ingredients and blend gently; leaving some small chunks is fine. Taste and adjust seasoning with more pepper sauce, salt and pepper if desired.

Cocktail Meatballs

According to southern tradition, the hostess at a ladies' luncheon should serve little meatballs in a chafing dish or a platter with toothpicks as a satisfying snack for any men in attendance. Husband #3's Paternal Grandmother came up with this recipe. It's pretty awesome.

Whatcha Need:

White sandwich bread, 5 slices (I use rye bread because I prefer it but you use whatever you like)
1 cup milk 3 large eggs, beaten
1 small white onion, minced
1 tbsp salt
2 tsps sweet paprika
1 tsp dry mustard
1/2 tsp freshly ground black pepper
1/2 tsp ground mace
1 and 1/2 lbs lean ground turkey
1/2 lb of ground pork Vegetable oil, for brushing
1 cup ketchup
1/2 cup currant jelly
1/2 cup dry sherry
1 tbsp Worcestershire sauce

How To Do It:

Preheat the broiler. In a large bowl, soak the bread in the milk for 1 minute, until softened. Squeeze out the excess milk and return the bread to the bowl. Add the eggs, onion, salt, paprika, dry mustard, pepper and mace and mix until smooth. Add the ground meat and mix until evenly combined. Brush a large rimmed baking sheet with oil. Using a 2 tbsp-size ice cream scoop, form the meat into 1/2-inch balls; roll until smooth. Transfer the meatballs to the baking sheet and brush the tops with oil. Broil 10 inches from the heat for about 10 minutes, shifting the sheet occasionally, until the meatballs are sizzling and browned. Meanwhile, in a large, deep skillet, combine the ketchup, jelly, sherry and Worcestershire. Add 1/2 cup of water and bring to a simmer, whisking until the jelly is melted. Using a slotted spoon, add the meatballs to the sauce and simmer over low heat until thickly glazed, about 15 minutes. Transfer the meatballs to a bowl and serve with toothpicks.

California Style Pizza

You can make crust or, use an already made crust and then a almost "made" crust... The toppings vary but I've had much luck with this white sauce pizza with typical California toppings...
Sun-dried tomato, grilled chicken, fresh basil, asparagus or artichoke and pepper jack cheese.

Whatcha Need:
For the Crust:
1 (.25 oz) package active dry yeast 1 cup warm water (110 degrees tap water temp...no hotter because it'll kill the yeast) 2 cups bread flour 2 tbsps olive oil 1 tsp salt 2 tsps white sugar
Pizza Toppings:
1 X 16 oz can of tomato puree, (or 2 cups of my super Quick Tomato Sauce in the Sauce Chapter),
1 X 16 oz jar of Alfredo Sauce (depending on which one is your fav!)
1 bunch fresh basil
2 cups grilled, shredded chicken breast meat
2 cups sun dried tomatoes, julienned
2 X 16 oz can of artichoke hearts, drained
1 16 oz package of turkey pepperoni
8 asparagus spears

How To Do It:

In a small bowl, dissolve yeast in warm water. Let stand until creamy, about 10 minutes. In a large bowl, combine 2 cups bread flour, olive oil, salt, white sugar and the yeast mixture; stir well to combine. Beat well until a stiff dough has formed.
Cover and rise until doubled in volume, about 30 minutes.

Meanwhile, preheat oven to 350 degrees F. Turn dough out onto a well floured surface. Form dough into a round and roll out into a pizza crust shape. Cover with your favorite sauce and toppings and bake in preheated oven until golden brown, about 20 minutes.

Blue Cheesecake

Yep, a blue cheese "cheesecake". Great for a centerpiece. Add some candies pecans or walnuts on top and it's a wonderful spread for crusty bread or rice crackers.

Whatcha Need:

(8 ounce) packages cream cheese
2 cups blue cheese, crumbled
1 cup sour cream
1/3 tsp ground white pepper
4 eggs
1/4 cups sour cream
1 red bell pepper, halved, seeds removed
1 green onion

How To Do It:

Preheat oven to 300 degrees F.

Beat cream cheese and blue cheese in large mixing bowl until light and fluffy--about 5 minutes. Mix in 1 cup sour cream and pepper. Add eggs - one at a time - mixing well after each addition. Pour mixture into buttered 9 inch spring-form pan. Bake 60 - 65 minutes or until wooden pick inserted near center comes out clean. Remove from oven and let stand 5 minutes. Carefully spread 1 1/4 cup sour cream over top. Return to oven 5 minutes. Cool completely on wire rack. Refrigerate several hours or overnight.

To serve, place on serving plate. Carefully remove sides of pan. Decorate top with red pepper cut into flower shapes with small cookie cutter and green onion tops as stems.

Caprese

I love making this. It's really pretty and deeeeelish!

Whatcha Need:

cup aged balsamic vinegar
6 fresh, ripe Roma tomatoes, cut into-inch slices
(about 1 lb or 2 cups sliced)
12 oz fresh mozzarella cheese, cut into-inch slices
1/2 cup loosely packed fresh basil leaves
Extra Virgin Olive Oil (to taste)

How To Do It:

Heat a small saucepan over medium heat 1 minute or until hot. Add vinegar, bring to a simmer, and cook 5 minutes or until vinegar is reduced to cup and coats the back of a spoon. Remove from heat.
(Vinegar can be prepared up to 1 day ahead.) Alternate tomato and mozzarella slices on a large serving platter. Stack basil leaves, and roll up tightly beginning at 1 long side; cut basil crosswise into thin strips or, if using small leaves, leave whole. Arrange basil over tomato and mozzarella slices. Drizzle desired amount of reduced balsamic vinegar over salad.

Serve salad right away.

Spinach Artichoke Dip

A great summertime dip!

Whatcha Need:

1 cup thawed, chopped frozen spinach
1.5 cups thawed, chopped frozen artichoke hearts
6 ounces cream cheese
1/4 cup sour cream
1/4 cup mayonnaise
1/3 cup grated Parmesan
1/2 tsp red pepper flakes
1/4 tsp salt
1/4 tsp garlic powder

How To Do It:

Boil spinach and artichokes in 1 cup of water until tender and drain. Discard liquid.

Heat cream cheese in microwave for 1 minute or until hot and soft. Stir in rest of ingredients and serve hot.

Yep, its that simple!!! Serve with blue or white corn tortilla chips.

Chapter Three

SAUCES

BBQ Sauce of the Gods

There are as many different BBQ sauces on the planet as there are the people who claim that theirs is "the only one worth having!" this is mine. You be the judge.

Whatcha Need:
1 large onion, chopped 6 garlic cloves, peeled
1 pickled jalapeño pepper, seeded and chopped
2 tsps of Chipotle chili powder
1 Tbsp tomato paste
2 Tbsp Dijon mustard
3/4 cup distilled white vinegar
1/4 cup Spiced Rum
1 tsp paprika
1/3 cup ketchup
2 tsps Worcestershire sauce
1/4 cup light brown sugar
1 bay leaf
Salt

How To Do It:

Purée all of the sauce ingredients except the bay leaf, in a blender until smooth. 2 Put sauce and bay leaf into a large pot and add 1 quart of water. Bring mixture to a boil. Let the sauce boil down until it has been reduced by two thirds. Salt to taste. Remove bay leaf before serving.

Alfredo Sauce

This original version of the famed pasta sauce has a great backstory. Alfredo di Ielio was a restaurateur in Rome in 1914. When his wife was pregnant with their second child she had no appetite and her health was failing. Alfredo created this special sauce for pasta, just for her.

Whatcha Need:

1 lb fresh very thin fettuccine
6 ounces unsalted butter
6 ounces parmigiano-reggiano cheese, grated (aged 24 months)

How To Do It:
Cook the fettuccine noodles in 1 gallon of salted boiling water for three minutes.
At the same time, mix the butter at room temperature in a bowl with the grated cheese until the cheese almost dissolves, forming a smooth cream.
Strain the pasta leaving just a small amount of water and toss the noodles with the Alfredo sauce. As I lover of cheese, I always sprinkle additional grated cheese on top.

Pink Vodka Sauce

People just can't seem to get enough of this one!

Whatcha Need:

2 tbsp olive oil
2 tbsp butter
1/2 cup minced shallot
1 cup canned crushed tomatoes
1/2 cup heavy cream
1 tsp salt
1 tsp black pepper
1/3 cup vodka

How To Do It:

In a large skillet, heat the oil and butter over medium heat until the butter melts.
Add the shallot and sauté' until tender but not browned, about 2 minutes. Add the crushed tomatoes, cream, salt, and pepper. Cook for 1 minute, stirring occasionally.

Add the vodka and continue cooking for 2 minutes, stirring occasionally, until the vodka evaporates slightly and the sauce thickens. Serve over pasta of your choice, or you can always do what I do and dunk cheesy garlic bread in it!

Tomato Salsa

Did you know that salsa is the number 1 condiment in the united states? True. For the longest time, ketchup held on to that honor but over the years as ethnic foods became more of a main stay, salsa was promoted to numero uno!

Whatcha Need:

1 small red onion, chopped
1/2 tsp salt
Juice of 2 limes
1/4 tsp sugar
red or green jalapeño chilies, seeded and finely chopped
4 medium tomatoes, chopped
1 cup fresh or frozen (thawed) corn kernels
1 cup chopped cilantro

How To Do It:

Place the chopped onion in a bowl, sprinkle with the salt, squeeze the lime juice over and set aside for 15 to 20 minutes.

Add the sugar, chopped chilies, tomatoes, corn, and cilantro to the onion mixture and stir. Cover tightly and chill for 1 hour before using. If you refrigerate over night, even better!

Chocolate Port Dessert Sauce

You could pour this sauce over anything (and i mean anything, not that i recommend an old leather boot for dessert) and say, "what a magical sauce!"

Whatcha Need:

3/4 cup whipping cream
1/4 cup whole milk
1/4 cup (1/2 stick) unsalted butter
8 ounces bittersweet or semisweet chocolate, chopped
1/4 cup tawny Port

How To Do It:

Bring whipping cream, whole milk, and unsalted butter to simmer in small heavy saucepan. Remove saucepan from heat and add chopped chocolate.

Whisk mixture until smooth. Stir in tawny Port. (Sauce can be made 2 days ahead. Cover and chill. Warm over medium-low heat before serving.)

Gorgonzola Sauce

I have made this sauce so many times I can't even count!

Whatcha Need:

2 cups heavy whipping cream
1/3 cup crumbly Gorgonzola (about 3 tbsp more if you are really a fan of this cheese like me!)
3 tbsp freshly grated Parmigiano reggiano
1 tsp ground Anise seed (you can use the whole seed if you really like the flavor)
3/4 tsp black pepper
2 tbsp freshly chopped parsley
1/4 tsp kosher salt

How To Do It:

Slowly and with love, bring the cream to a boil. Reduce heat to medium low and add all the other ingredients.

Cook until thickened and reduced by half.

Hollandaise

Once thought to be an impossible sauce to perfect, you'll be very surprised at how simple it really is to create the perfect hollandaise... The trick? Patience.

Whatcha Need:

3 egg yolks
1 1/2 tbsp fresh lemon juice
4 tbsp unsalted butter, chilled
3/4 cup unsalted butter, melted
salt to taste
1 tsp ground white pepper

How To Do It:

Add egg yolks to a small saucepan; whisk until lemon yellow and slightly thick, about 1 minute. Whisk in lemon juice. Add 2 tbsps cold butter, and place over very low heat. Whisk constantly while butter is melting, and continue whisking until thick enough to see the pan between strokes.

Remove pan from heat, and beat in 1 tbsp cold butter. Repeat. Whisk in melted butter a little bit at a time all the while whisking the living life out of the mixture. Season with salt and white pepper to taste.

Pesto!

I love pesto, i'm not gonna lie... I love it! I would take pesto to Prom if given the chance to ask it.

Whatcha Need:

2/3 cup packed, coarsely chopped fresh basil
1/3 cup grated Parmesan cheese
1/3 cup olive oil
2 tbsp pine nuts or sunflower kernels
1/2 tsp salt
1/8 tsp pepper
1 clove garlic, peeled

How To Do It:
(yes, its just this easy)

In a food processor or blender, combine all the ingredients; cover and process until blended.

Cover and freeze for up to 3 months.

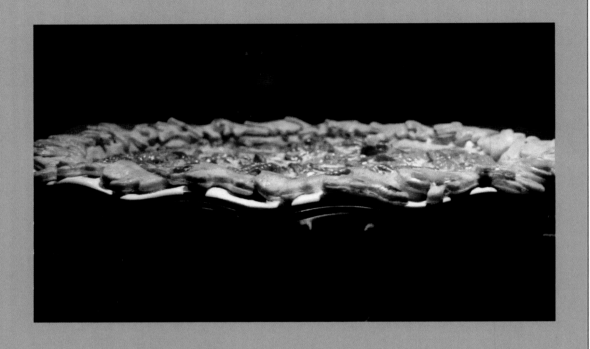

Chapter Four

DESSERTS

I could never understand why dessert was always left until the very end of the meal.

It was thought to have originated from the custom of removing the aftertaste of a meal with a sweet taste, desserts leave a mouth sweet-tasting and revitalized.

The confection derives its name from the French word desservir, which literally means to clear the table. Today there are literally thousands of dessert varieties. Some popular sweet desserts that have been around since ancient times include cakes, pies and ice cream like you didnt know that.

Now, onto Pie 101. Did you know the roots of pie, as a dessert, originated in the Neolithic period beginning in 9500 b.c.? Yep, known as galettes, these free-form pies contained different grains and honey. Galettes baked over hot coals. Pastry originated as bakers added fruit, nuts and honey to bread dough to serve to the pharaoh (1304-1237 b.c.). Drawings of this practice decorate the tomb walls of King Ramses ii. Pie-making techniques and ingredients often changed because of different conditions and ingredients.

The pilgrim women brought their favorite family pie recipes to America to use as desserts. They used traditional pie fillings and incorporated berries and fruits that the native Americans used as they adapted to the new world.

Colonial women started the tradition of using round pans for pies. This tradition came about to conserve ingredients. The women used flattened pies and then laid rolled out pastry over the top of the pan and cut off the corners. Pies became a part of American culture in the 1700s as pioneer women served pie as a dessert with every meal. As an evening meal, apple pie became a popular dessert with American children.

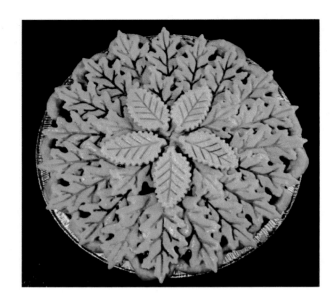

Old Faithful Pie Crust

Whatcha Need:

2 1/2 cups all-purpose flour
1 tsp salt
1 cup (2 sticks) cold ,unsalted butter, cut into 1/2-inch
pieces
1/4 to 1/2 cup ice water

How To Do It:

Pulse flour and salt in a food processor. Add butter, and pulse until mixture forms coarse crumbs with some larger pieces remaining, about 10 seconds.
With machine running, add ice water in a slow, steady stream just until dough holds together without being wet or sticky, no longer than 30 seconds.

Divide dough in half, and shape into disks. Wrap in plastic; refrigerate at least 1 hour or overnight. Dough can be frozen up to 1 month; thaw in the refrigerator overnight before using.

Chocolate Peppermint Torte

Peppermint and chocolate together again!

Whatcha Need:

2 cups chopped semi-sweet chocolate
3/4 cup butter
1/3 cup cocoa powder
1 tsp instant espresso powder
5 eggs
1 cup minus 1 tbsp granulated sugar
1 tbsp all-purpose flour
1/8 tsp. peppermint extract
3 candy canes, crushed
Powdered sugar for dusting

How To Do It:

Preheat the oven to 350F. Lightly butter 9-inch spring form pan and set aside. In medium saucepan, melt the chocolate and butter over the lowest heat. Mix in the cocoa powder and espresso powders until smooth and set aside for a few minutes to cool. While the chocolate is cooling, whisk together the eggs, sugar, and flour until they are completely combined and foamy. Fold the egg mixture into the chocolate until the color is uniform and pour the batter into the prepared pan.
Bake for 45 minutes, until a toothpick pulls out moist crumbs when inserted near the center of the torte. Allow the cake to cool in the pan on a rack for 15 minutes. Run a knife or inverted spatula along the edges of the torte and loosen the sides of the pan. Cool for 5 minutes and remove the sides of the pan. Invert the cake an a platter and cool completely before serving. Spinkle crushed candy canes on top or if using berries, arrange berries and dust with powdered sugar.
This chocolate torte recipe makes 10 servings.

Classic Creme Brulee

It is said that if you make this for dessert the very first time a potential mate has dinner at your house, they will be yours forever; or so I'm to understand.

Whatcha Need:

6 egg yolks
6 tbsps white sugar, divided
1/2 tsp vanilla extract
2 1/2 cups heavy cream
2 tbsps brown sugar
2 tbsps Grand Marnier

*side note: if you don't have a double boiler you can use a stainless steel bowl over a saucepan of simmering water. USE CAUTION since the bowl will be very hot!

How To Do It:
Preheat oven to 300 degrees F (150 degrees C).
Beat egg yolks, 4 tbsp sugar and vanilla in a mixing bowl until thick and creamy. Add Grand Marnier at this point.
Pour cream into a saucepan and stir over low heat until it almost comes to boil. Remove the cream from heat immediately. Stir cream into the egg yolk mixture; beat until combined. Pour cream mixture into the top of a double boiler. Stir over simmering water until mixture lightly coats the back of a spoon; approximately 3 minutes. Remove mixture from heat immediately and pour into a shallow heat-proof dish or individual Ramekins. Bake in preheated oven for 25 minutes. Remove from oven and cool to room temperature. Refrigerate for 1 hour, or overnight. Next, preheat oven to broil (or you can use your kitchen blow torch everyone has one, right?) In a small bowl combine remaining 2 tbsp white sugar and brown sugar. Sift this mixture evenly over custard. Place dish under broiler until sugar melts, about 2 minutes. Watch carefully so as not to burn.
Remove from heat and allow to cool.

Refrigerate until custard is set again before serving.

Nanaimo Bars

A very popular Canadian dessert square.
Yield 24 bars.

Whatcha Need:
Bottom Layer ***
1/2 cup unsalted butter (super important you use unsalted butter my friends)
1/4 cup sugar
5 tbsps cocoa
1 egg beaten
1 1/4 cup graham wafer crumbs
1/2 cup finely chopped almonds
1 cup coconut
Second Layer *
1/2 cup unsalted butter
2 tbsps cream PLUS
2 tsps cream
2 tbsps vanilla custard powder
2 cups icing sugar
***Third Layer ***
4 squares semi-sweet chocolate (1 oz. each)
2 tbsps unsalted butter

How To Do It:

Bottom Layer...
Melt first 3 ingredients in top of double boiler. Add egg and stir to cook and thicken.
Remove from heat. Stir in crumbs, coconut, and nuts. Press firmly into an un-greased
8" x 8" pan.
Second Layer...

Cream butter, cream, custard powder, and icing sugar together well. Beat until light.
Spread over bottom layer.
Third Layer...

Melt chocolate and butter over low heat. Cool. Once cool, but still liquid, pour over second layer and chill in refrigerator.

The Lemon Cake

Cardamom makes this very special.

Whatcha Need:

1/2 cup unsalted butter, softened but not melted
1 1/2 cups unbleached flour
1 tsp baking powder
1/4 tsp baking soda
1/2 tsp salt
3/4 cup granulated sugar
3 tbsp grated lemon zest (2 tbsp for the cake batter and 1 tbsp for the glaze, that comes later)
6 tbsp fresh lemon juice (you can either use juice from the lemons you just zested above OR, any fresh lemon juice from your favorite food shop).
3/4 tsp ground cardamom (OR, since this spice costs about a billion dollars in most stores, you can use 1/2 tsp of ground cinnamon and 1/4 tsp of ground nutmeg)
2 large eggs
1/2 cup sour cream (liquid measure)
1 1/2 cups icing/ confectioner sugar

How To Do It:
(pre-heat your oven to 375F)
Sift, yep, SIFT the flour, baking powder, baking soda, salt and spices together in a medium bowl. In a standing mixer or large bowl with a hand held mixer (yeah, you can use a wooden spoon too if you want to build up your forearms!) Beat butter, granulated sugar and 2 tbsp of lemon zest until its light and fluffy. Add eggs one at a time until totally mixed in then add 3 tbsp of lemon juice and sour cream. Reduce mixer speed to the lowest setting and add the flour mixture until just combined then pour batter into a buttered and floured 8 spring-form cake pan. Bake for 30 minutes (most ovens 30 minutes will be perfect timing. You can always check doneness by inserting a wooden toothpick into the centre of the cake if it comes out clean then consider it done!)
Let the cake cool for about 10 minutes before turning it out onto a wire rack to completely cool. Now its time to make the glaze. In a small bowl whisk together 3 tbsp lemon juice, 1 1/2 cups of icing/confectioners sugar and 1 tbsp lemon zest. Starting in the very centre of the cake, pour the glaze on the top and let drizzle down the sides.

There you have it ! Bob's your Uncle and DONE!

Super Wicked Chocolate Brownie

This is the recipe that started it all! (dedicated to my good friend, Ric Keeley. How many pans of these have we made over the years? I love you dearly.)

Whatcha Need:

1 sticks (3/4 cup) unsalted butter
5 oz. Unsweetened chocolate, coarsely chopped
2 cups granulated sugar
1 tbsp espresso powder or instant
coffee granules
1 tsp pure vanilla
1/4 tsp salt
4 large eggs, lightly beaten
1 cup unbleached flour
 cup bittersweet chocolate chips

How To Do It:

(pre-heat oven to 375F)
Line a 13X9 1 baking pan with foil, allowing about 2 of foil to hang over the ends of the pan. Grease foil well with 1 tbsp of butter.
Melt remaining butter with the chocolate in a glass/ microwave proof bowl at :30 second intervals (stirring after each) until mixture is smooth. Let cool for 5 minutes then transfer to medium sized bowl and whisk in sugar, espresso powder, vanilla and salt. Add eggs one at a time and whisk until batter is smooth. Stir in flour until combined.
Spread batter evenly in prepared baking pan and bake in the middle of the oven until the top is firm and edges have just begin the pull away from the sides of the pan (about 20 minutes DO NOT OVERBAKE).
Let cool for 10 minutes then, carefully very carefully, lift brownies from pan by grasping both ends of foil and set on cooling rack an additional 10 minutes or until brownies are completely cooled.

(This is the base brownie recipe you can add anything you like, for example swirl peanut butter into the batter once you spread it into baking pan or, drizzle caramel sauce on top before bakingdrag a knife through to pull the caramel sauce into cool patterns. You can add pretty much anything, well except perhaps for trout!)

Apple Sharlotka

Delicious with any type of apple (in my opinion). This is a huge favorite for Hanukkah.

Whatcha Need:

4 Granny Smith apples peeled, cored, quartered and thinly sliced
1 tbsp fresh lemon juice
1 cup sugar
3/4 cup plus 2 tbsps all-purpose flour
1/4 tsp ground cinnamon
1/4 tsp freshly grated nutmeg
Pinch of kosher salt
3 large eggs

How To Do It:

Preheat the oven to 350. Grease the bottom and side of an 8-inch spring-form pan.
In a large bowl, toss the apples with the lemon juice and 2 tbsps of the sugar and let stand for 15 minutes.

Meanwhile, in a small bowl, whisk the flour with the cinnamon, nutmeg and salt. In a medium bowl, using an electric mixer, beat the eggs with the almond extract and the remaining 3/4 cup plus 2 tbsps sugar at medium-high speed until thick and pale yellow and a ribbon forms when the beaters are lifted, 8 to 10 minutes. Gently fold in the dry ingredients just until incorporated. Spread the apples in the prepared pan in an even layer, then pour the batter evenly over them. Let stand for 5 minutes to allow the batter to sink in a little.

Bake the Sharlotka for about 1 hour, until it is golden and crisp on top and a cake tester inserted in the center comes out clean. Transfer to a rack and let rest for 15 minutes. Unmold and transfer to a serving platter. Dust with confectioners sugar and serve warm.

Almond Torte

Every time I make this it seems that angels sing! It's so simple and so darn good.

Whatcha Need:
1/2 cup softened, unsalted butter
7 oz almond paste (1 tube, cut into small pieces)
3 large eggs
1/4 tsp Amaretto
1/2 tsp Triple Sec
1 tsp baking powder
1 cup unbleached, all-purpose flour
Some powdered sugar for dusting

How To Do It:
Preheat your oven to 350F. Spray with baking spray and dust with flour an 8 inch round pan (you can use a spring form pan too if you have one handy). Using either a standing mixer or heck, even a hand mixer will work, cream butter and sugar till fluffy (about 3 minutes).

Add almond paste as the mixer still whirls to blend it all in. Then, add eggs one at a time and make sure they are mixed in super well.

Beat in Amaretto and Triple Sec... or "the booze" as I like to call it.

Slow your standing mixer down to the first setting and fold in the baking powder and flour.

Pour batter into prepared pan and bake about 45 minutes. Remove from oven and let cool for 10 minutes. Flip it onto a cooling rack (upside down) until it's completely cooled. Dust with powdered sugar or, you can do what I do and flood the darn thing on top with caramel sauce OR, make a simple glaze from 1.5 cups of powdered sugar and 3 tbsp of fresh lemon juice. Pour glaze over torte and let harden.

Chocolate Pie

"I don't want any chocolate pie", said no one ever.

Whatcha Need:

1 Fully baked 9 pie crust (see recipe for Old Faithful Pie Crust)
4 cups heavy whipping cream
 cup cornstarch
1 cup granulated sugar
5 oz. semisweet chocolate chips
2 tsps pure vanilla extract

How To Do It:

Combine 1/2 cup of the cream with cornstarch in either a small glass bowl or measuring cup and stir carefully to make a rather paste. In a large nonstick saucepan pour the remaining 3.5 cups of heavy cream, the paste, sugar, chocolate chips and vanilla. Stir until well blended (I used a whisk for this task) over low heat until the chocolate chips melt completely. Cook until the mixture becomes very thick, all the while stirring make sure it doesnt burn or stick to the bottom of the pan. After about the 25 minutes remove from the heat and pour the pudding into a large bowl.

Cover with plastic wrap, pressing lightly down on the surface of the pudding to prevent a skin from forming. Let pudding cool to room temperature.
Pour into prepared pie crust and chill for two hours or overnight. Serve with whipped cream and chocolate shavings.

Chapter Five

VEGETARIAN?
No Problem.

Artichoke and Eggplant Panini

Artichoke and Eggplant Panini
Everyone has a version of this one. I find that this turns out so much better when it's actually grilled and not baked or fried... Prepare a gas grill for direct-heat cooking over medium-high heat. It's remarkably filling and deeeelish!

<u>Whatcha Need:</u>
1 (6 1/2-ounces) jar marinated artichokes, drained and chopped
2 tbsps mayonnaise
1 tbsp drained capers
1 small garlic clove
1 (3/4-pound) eggplant
5 tbsps olive oil, divided
1 (1-pound) round loaf Italian bread, 8 (1/3-inch-thick) slices cut from middle
1/4 pound Fontina (preferably Italian), thinly sliced

<u>How To Do It:</u>
Pulse artichokes, mayonnaise, capers, and garlic in a food processor until coarsely chopped. Trim off a thin slice from 2 opposite long sides of eggplant then, cut eggplant lengthwise into 4 (1/3-inchthick) slices. Brush both sides of slices with 2 tbsps oil (total) and season with 1/4 tsp each of salt and pepper. Grill eggplant slices, covered, turning once and brushing grilled sides with 1 tbsp oil (total), until golden-brown and tender, about 4 minutes, then transfer to a tray. Brush both sides of bread with remaining 2 tbsps oil and grill, covered, without turning, until grill marks appear, about 2 minutes. Top each of 4 bread slices, grilled sides up, with cheese and an eggplant slice. Spread artichoke mixture on remaining 4 bread slices, grilled sides up, then assemble sandwiches. Put sandwiches on grill and press down with a metal spatula, then grill, turning once, until heated through and grill marks appear, about 4 minutes total.

Carrot & Spring Pea Risotto

Whatcha Need:

4 cups vegetable stock
2 cups fresh carrot juice
2 tbsps extra-virgin olive oil
1 large shallot, finely chopped
1 1/2 cups arborio rice (10 ounces)
1/2 cup dry white wine
2 1/2 tbsps white wine vinegar
1/2 cup freshly grated
Parmigiano-Reggiano cheese
2 tbsps unsalted butter
Salt
Freshly ground pepper
1 cup frozen baby peas (or if in season,
fresh Spring peas)

How To Do It:

In a medium saucepan, bring the vegetable stock and carrot juice to a simmer; keep warm. In a large saucepan, heat the olive oil. Add the shallot and cook over moderate heat, stirring, until softened, about 4 minutes. Add the rice and cook, stirring, until slightly milky colored, about 1 minute. Add the wine and 2 tbsps of the vinegar and cook, stirring, until the liquid is absorbed.

Stir in the hot stock mixture, 1 cup at a time, stirring constantly and adding more stock once it has been absorbed, about 20 minutes total; the rice should be al dente and suspended in a thick, creamy sauce. Add the cheese and 1 tbsp of the butter, season with salt and pepper and stir until creamy. In a medium skillet, melt the remaining 1 tbsp of butter. Add the peas, season with salt and pepper and cook over moderately high heat until warmed through, about 1 minute. Add the remaining 1/2 tbsp of vinegar to the peas, then fold into the risotto.

Serve immediately.

Dr. Wanner's Rice & Beans

Whatcha Need:

2 cups brown or white rice (cooked per package instructions)
1 tbsp olive oil
1 small onion, chopped
1/2 green bell pepper, thinly sliced
1/2 red bell pepper, thinly sliced (for added flavor you can substitute roasted red bell peppers or some chopped pimentos)
3 cloves minced garlic
2 16-ounce cans of black beans, rinsed and drained
2 Tbsp white vinegar
A few dashes of Tabasco or 1/4 teaspoon cayenne powder
1 teaspoon dried oregano or 1 heaping Tbsp chopped fresh oregano
Salt and pepper to taste
Optional Lime wedges and cilantro for garnish (I always go for the "options").

How To Do It:

Clean and Chop the peppers and the onion but keep the peppers separate from the onion.

In a large sauté pan, add olive oil to coat the bottom of the pan. Once at a medium to medium/high heat add the peppers. Stir regularly so they don't burn. Add the spices. If it gets dry add a few tablespoons of water.

Once the peppers are sautéed remove to bowl. Add more olive oil to pan and once heated add onion and saute until translucent. You may want to add more spices at this point. It all depends on how much heat you want.

Take one can of beans and rinse in strainer thoroughly. Take second can of beans and rinse lightly in the can. Take third can of beans and only drain off a slight amount of fluid.
Add peppers back to saute pan with onion. Add beans and stir all ingredients together. Allow all the ingredients to simmer for 10 to 15 minutes.

You may add moisture with just some water or white wine if necessary.

Eggplant Parmesan with a Twist!

Whatcha Need:

For Tomato Sauce:
2 tbsps olive oil
1 small onion, finely chopped
1 garlic clove, minced
1 (14-ounce) can whole tomatoes in juice
1/2 cup water
1/2 tsp sugar
3 tbsps finely chopped basil

For Eggplant Stacks:
2 (1-pound) eggplants
6 tbsps olive oil, divided, plus additional for drizzling
3/4 cup plain dry bread crumbs
1/2 cup grated Parmigiano-Reggiano
1/2 cup finely chopped flat-leaf parsley
2 garlic cloves, minced, divided
6 large eggs, lightly beaten
1/2 cup water
1/4 tsp hot red-pepper flakes
1/2 pound arugula, coarse stems discarded, coarsely chopped
1 cup packed basil leaves, coarsely chopped
1/2 pound cold fresh mozzarella, ends trimmed and remainder cut into 4 (1/2-inch-thick) slices

How To Do It:

Make tomato sauce:
Heat oil in a heavy medium saucepan over medium heat until it shimmers, then cook onion and garlic, stirring occasionally, until softened, about 6 minutes.
Meanwhile, blend tomatoes with juice in a blender until almost smooth. Add to onion mixture in saucepan with water, sugar, and 1/4 tsp salt and simmer, partially covered, stirring occasionally, until slightly thickened, about 10 minutes. Stir in basil and keep warm, covered.

Bake eggplant:
Preheat oven to 450°F with rack in lowest position.
Cut 12 (1/3-inch-thick) rounds from widest portion of eggplants. Brush both sides with 2 tbsps oil and season with 1/2 tsp salt (total). Bake on an oiled baking sheet, turning once, until golden and tender, 20 to 30 minutes. Transfer to a plate and keep warm, covered. Leave oven on.

Make egg patties and sauté arugula:
Stir together bread crumbs, parmesan, parsley, half of garlic, and 1/4 tsp each of salt and pepper, then stir in eggs and water.
Heat 3 tbsps oil in a 12-inch heavy skillet over medium heat until it shimmers. Drop 4 rounded 1/3 cups of egg mixture into skillet and cook, turning once, until patties are golden brown and puffed, about 5 minutes. Transfer to paper towels to drain.
Add remaining tbsp oil to skillet and cook remaining garlic with red-pepper flakes, stirring, until garlic is golden, about 30 seconds.
Add arugula and basil and stir until just wilted, then stir in 1/8 tsp salt.

Assemble stacks:
Arrange 4 egg patties about 3 inches apart on a baking sheet. Top each with 2 Tbsp tomato sauce, 1 slice mozzarella, 1 eggplant slice, 2 more tbsps tomato sauce, another eggplant slice, arugula mixture, and remaining eggplant. Bake until cheese melts, 5 to 10 minutes.
Drizzle with additional oil and serve remaining sauce on the side.

Lebanese Mjadra

Whatcha Need:

2 cup red lentils (brown)
½ cup olive oil
1 cup cooked corn
1 red bell pepper (diced)
2 cup long grain rice (cooked)
1 medium onion
2 cup vegetable stock
2 heads butter lettuce
2 lemons (seeded and cut into wedges)

How To Do It:

Using a medium saucepan, bring lentils and 4 cups of water to the boil on a high heat. Cover, reduce the heat to medium and simmer for 20 minutes.

Meanwhile, heat oil in a frying pan. Cook the onion for 5 minutes, until soft and golden. Add half of the onion to the lentils. Also add the rice and stock. Season with salt. Return to the boil and cook for another 20 minutes, until thick and creamy.

With the remaining half of the onion -- continue to fry for another 10 minutes. It should be dark brown and caramelized.

Add the caramelized onion, corn and red bell pepper to the lentils and cook another 5 minutes. Stir occasionally.

To serve- spoon lentils into lettuce cups and serve with lemon wedges, pepper and yogurt if desired.

Spicy Eggplant & Green Bean

I love this dish. You just can't go wrong!

<u>Whatcha Need:</u>

5 tablespoons vegetable oil, divided
4 garlic cloves, chopped
1 tablespoon chopped peeled fresh ginger
1 (14- to 16-ounce) eggplant, peeled, cut into 2 x 1/2 x 1/2-inch sticks
8 ounces green beans, trimmed, cut into 2-inch pieces
1 tablespoon grated lime peel
1 teaspoon Thai green curry paste
1 cup canned unsweetened coconut milk
3 green onions, chopped
1/4 cup chopped fresh cilantro
2 tablespoons chopped fresh mint
(Brown Rice – enough to serve 8, cooked and kept warm)

<u>How To Do It:</u>

This is a delicious vegetarian entrée for two or more — just add rice. You can find curry paste and coconut milk in the Asian foods section of the grocery store.

Heat 4 tablespoons oil in large skillet over medium-high heat. Add garlic and ginger; stir 30 seconds. Add eggplant and green beans. Cook until almost tender, stirring often, about 10 minutes. Cover and cook until completely tender, about 3 minutes longer.

Transfer vegetables to bowl.

Add 1 tablespoon oil, lime peel, and curry paste to same skillet; stir 15 seconds. Add coconut milk; bring to boil, whisking until smooth. Return vegetables to skillet; toss until sauce thickens enough to coat vegetables, about 3 minutes.

Season with salt. Mix in onions, cilantro, and mint.

TOOLS OF
THE TRADE

As someone who LOVES to be in the kitchen I always have these tools on hand:

The off-set spatula, our friend. How we have managed without this wonder in engineering for so many years I will never know!

Whisks. Every size whisk you can find. Heck, I carry a tiny whisk on my key chain; just in case. You never know when a whisk emergency might pop up.

No less than 8 wooden spoons.

Bowls glass bowls, ceramic bowls, stainless steel bowls, extra mixing bowls for your standing mixer, extra bowls for your food processor, little bowls to put stuff in, big deep bowls for folding meringues, heat resistant bowls, copper bowls (because they are pretty), and the list goes on.

Disposable piping bags. These are a must have item for a whole bunch of reasons aside from the obvious one; frosting cakes and cookies. How about piping mashed potatoes onto serving plates? How about for injecting custard into pas de choux for eclairs?

The Lemon Cake "all dressed up!"

Made in the USA
Las Vegas, NV
09 July 2023

74411604R00038